YOU ARE AN Amazing Boy

Inspiring Stories about Self Confidence, Courage, Creativity and Friendship

Phoebe Whimsy

COPYRIGHT © KHE LLC. All rights reserved.

No part of this book may be reproduced, distributed, or transmitted in any form or by any means, including photocopying, recording, or other electronic or mechanical methods, without the prior written permission of the author, except in the case of brief quotations embodied in critical reviews and certain other noncommercial uses permitted by copyright law.

LEGAL NOTICE

This is a work of fiction. Names, characters, places, and incidents either are products of the author's imagination or are used fictitiously. Any resemblance to actual persons, living or dead, or actual events is purely coincidental.
The author/publisher is not responsible for any errors or omissions, nor for any loss or damage caused or alleged to be caused directly or indirectly by following any advice or suggestions in this book.

DISCLAIMER NOTICE

The content of this book is intended for children and general reading purposes. While every effort has been made to ensure the content is suitable for a young audience, it is the responsibility of parents and guardians to assess the suitability of this book for their children. The author and publisher disclaim all liability for any harm or distress caused by the use or misuse of this material.

CONTENTS

Introduction	4
1. The Invisible Hero	5
2. The Courageous Climber	14
3. The Library Detective	22
4. The Art of Being Oliver	30
5. The Kindness Chain	36
6. The Forest Guardians	45
7. The Brave New Friend	54
8. The Magic of Saying Sorry	63
9. The Time Keeper	72
10. The Brave Listener	80
11. The Team Switcher	88
12. The Music Maker	96
Epilogue	105

Introduction

Welcome to *You are an Amazing Boy*, a collection of twelve inspiring stories about courage, kindness, and self-discovery. Each tale follows a young boy navigating challenges, finding his unique strengths, and making a positive impact on the world around him. From the secret acts of bravery in The Invisible Hero to the magical melodies of The Music Maker, these stories are filled with adventure, heart, and lessons that every boy can relate to and learn from.

This book celebrates the amazing qualities that make each boy unique—creativity, empathy, determination, and resilience. Whether it's overcoming fears in The Courageous Climber, standing up for fairness in The Team Switcher, or discovering the power of kindness in The Brave Listener, these stories remind us all that greatness lies in being true to ourselves. Get ready to embark on a journey of inspiration, and always remember: you are an amazing boy!

The Invisible Hero

1

The Invisible Hero

Ethan Bennett was a small, quiet boy with a big heart and an even bigger secret. He loved helping others but hated attention, which made him the perfect candidate for what would soon be an extraordinary adventure.

Ethan lived in the small, bustling town of Willow Creek, where he was often overlooked. His classmates didn't pick him for soccer games, and even his teachers sometimes forgot to call on him. But Ethan didn't mind too much. He liked observing the world around him—the joy, the struggles, and the little mysteries that made life interesting.

One rainy afternoon, Ethan sought refuge in his favorite place, the Willow Creek Antique Shop. The dimly lit store was packed with treasures from all corners of the world. There were old globes, dusty books, and curious trinkets that seemed to hold their own stories.

Ethan's fingers brushed against a smooth, silken fabric hanging near the back of the shop. It was a cloak—dark, shimmery, and unusually warm to the touch. Intrigued, he pulled it off the rack and draped it over his shoulders.

"Careful with that one," called Mr. Whitaker, the shop's elderly owner, from behind the counter. His kind eyes twinkled as he added, "It's special."

"What makes it special?" Ethan asked, tightening the cloak around him.

"You'll find out," Mr. Whitaker said cryptically. "But remember, power is best used for good."

Ethan chuckled nervously and decided to buy the cloak with the allowance he had saved. Little did he know that moment would change his life forever.

The First Disappearance

The following day, Ethan couldn't resist trying on the cloak again. He pulled it over his shoulders and adjusted the hood.

The second it slipped over his head, something strange happened. His reflection in the mirror disappeared.

"Whoa!" Ethan exclaimed, spinning around. His voice echoed in the empty room, but he couldn't see his hands, feet, or shadow. The cloak made him completely invisible.

His heart raced with excitement. He had always dreamed of doing something important, but his shyness held him back. Now, with the cloak, he could help others without anyone knowing it was him.

Ethan's Secret Mission

Ethan wasted no time putting his new ability to the test at school. He noticed Emma, the quiet girl who loved books, searching for her missing journal. She looked close to tears as she rummaged through her desk and backpack.

Ethan slipped on the cloak and became invisible. Moving silently through the classroom, he found her journal beneath a pile of papers on another desk. Carefully, he placed it on top of her books.

Facing the Bully

Word spread quickly around school about the mysterious "Invisible Helper." Ethan's classmates shared stories of how their lost items reappeared or doors opened when someone's hands were full. Everyone was curious, but no one could figure out who was behind it.

One day, Ethan noticed Liam, the school bully, picking on a younger boy named Toby in the playground. Liam snatched Toby's lunchbox and held it high above his head, laughing as Toby jumped and pleaded for it back.

Ethan felt a surge of anger. He pulled on the cloak and stepped into the fray. With a quick, invisible tug, he yanked the lunchbox out of Liam's hands. The bully looked around in confusion as the lunchbox floated in midair before landing gently in Toby's arms.

"What—?!" Liam stammered, his face pale. The other kids began whispering, their eyes wide.

"Thanks, Invisible Helper!" Toby shouted, clutching his lunchbox.

Liam, clearly spooked, backed away and didn't bother Toby again. Ethan felt a rush of satisfaction. The cloak had given him the confidence to stand up for others in a way he never could.

A Test of True Strength

Ethan continued his secret missions for weeks, helping classmates, fixing minor problems, and spreading kindness wherever he went. But one day, he faced a challenge that made him question everything.

The school held a talent show, and Ethan's best friend, Lucas, had signed up to perform a magic act. Lucas had been practicing for weeks, but his magic kit went missing on the day of the show.

Panicked, Lucas searched everywhere but couldn't find it. Ethan knew he could use the cloak to retrieve the kit, but there wasn't enough time before the show started.

"Ethan," Lucas said, his voice trembling, "I can't do this without my kit. I'll look like a fool."

Ethan hesitated. He wanted to help Lucas, but invisibility wouldn't solve the problem this time. He would have to step out of the shadows.

"Lucas," Ethan said, touching his friend's shoulder, "you don't need the kit. You've practiced enough—you've got this."

"But what if I mess up?" Lucas asked.

"I'll be right there cheering you on," Ethan replied. "No cloak, no tricks—just me."

Encouraged by Ethan's words, Lucas went on stage and performed a simple yet impressive routine with the tools he had. The audience cheered, and Lucas beamed with pride. Ethan realized that his true strength wasn't in the cloak but in his ability to support others with courage and kindness.

The Big Reveal

As the days passed, Ethan used the cloak less and less. He started speaking up in class, joining games at recess, and even helping friends openly. The confidence he had gained through his invisible acts of kindness now shone in everything he did.

One afternoon, Ethan returned to the antique shop to thank Mr. Whitaker.

"Ah, the cloak served you well, didn't it?" Mr. Whitaker asked with a knowing smile.

"It did," Ethan replied, handing the cloak back. "But I think someone else might need it more now."

Mr. Whitaker nodded, accepting the cloak. "Remember, Ethan, the real magic was never in the cloak. It was always in you."

Ethan left the shop feeling lighter than ever. He didn't need invisibility to make a difference—he only needed his heart and the courage to act.

The Legacy of the Invisible Hero
Word of the "Invisible Helper" eventually faded, but the impact of Ethan's actions lingered. His classmates were kinder, his school felt brighter, and Ethan had transformed. He was no longer the shy boy who stayed in the background. He was Ethan Bennett—the boy who proved that courage and kindness could change the world, one small act at a time.

And while no one knew the whole story, Ethan didn't mind. After all, true heroes don't need recognition. They need a willing heart.

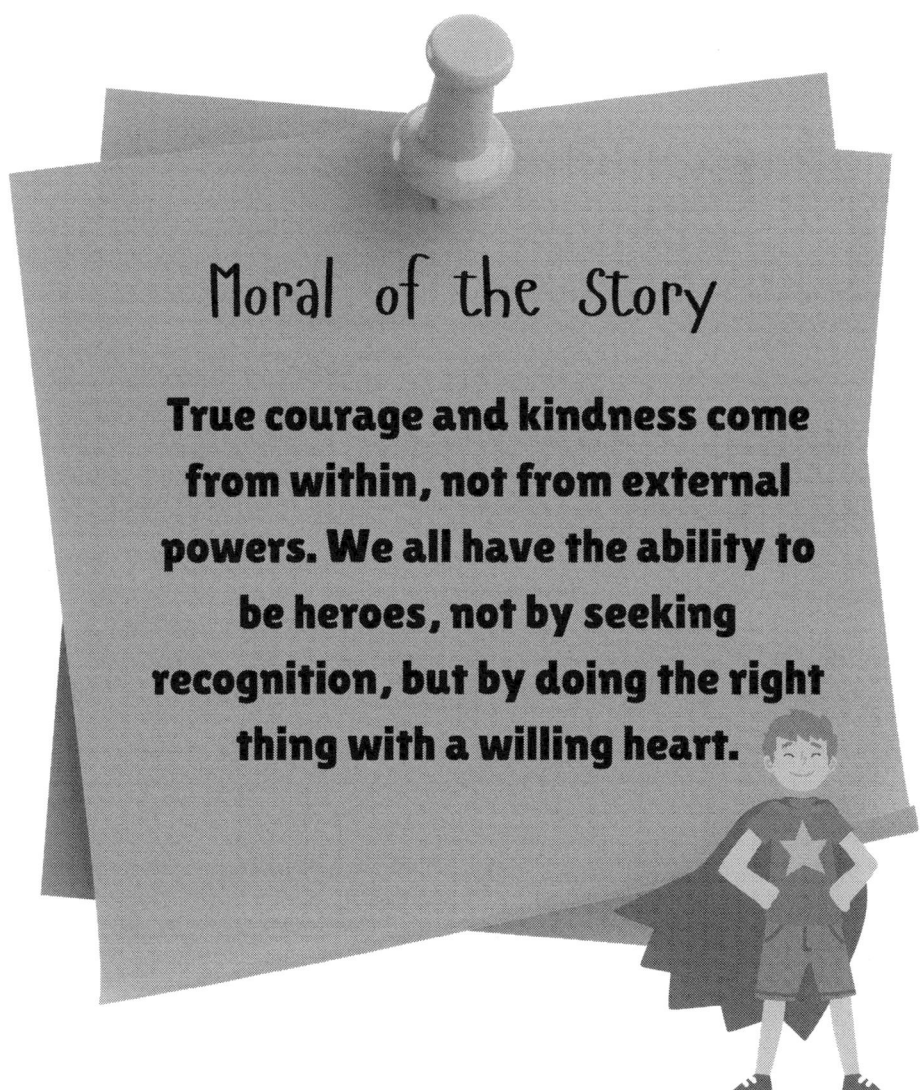

Moral of the Story

True courage and kindness come from within, not from external powers. We all have the ability to be heroes, not by seeking recognition, but by doing the right thing with a willing heart.

The Courageous Climber

2

The Courageous Climber

Liam Ferris was the kind of kid who loved being outdoors, but only with both feet planted firmly on the ground. He could outrun almost anyone in a game of tag and knew all the best spots to find frogs by the creek. But when it came to climbing? Forget it. Heights made him dizzy, and standing on a stool to reach the cookie jar felt like a daring adventure.

His friends, Milo and Theo, were the opposite. They always climbed trees, scaled rocks, and talked about big adventures. One day, they burst into Liam's backyard with a plan that sent a chill down his spine.

"Liam! You've got to come with us!" Milo said, bouncing with excitement.

"There's this awesome rock outcropping halfway up Ridge Hill," Theo added. "They say the view is amazing—like you can see the whole valley."

Liam froze. Ridge Hill was the tallest hill in their town, with jagged rocks and steep paths. "I don't think that's a good idea," he muttered, kicking at a pebble.

"Oh, come on!" Milo pleaded. "We'll do it together. We've done it before—it's not that bad."

Theo nudged Liam with a grin. "You'll never know how cool it is unless you try."

Liam hesitated. He didn't want to disappoint his friends, but the idea of climbing made his stomach churn. Finally, he sighed. "Okay. I'll try. But if I can't do it, don't laugh at me."

The Unexpected Trail

The boys set off the following day, carrying a small backpack with snacks and water. The base of Ridge Hill was easy enough, with a wide dirt trail winding through the woods. Birds chirped overhead, and the sunlight filtered through the leaves, creating dappled patterns on the ground.

"This isn't so bad," Liam thought as he followed Milo and Theo. "Maybe I can do this."

But then they reached the first challenge: a boulder blocking the trail. Milo scrambled up quickly, and Theo followed, grinning. Liam stared at the boulder, his heart pounding. It wasn't tall—maybe a little taller than he was—but it looked enormous.

"You can do it," Theo said, holding out a hand. "Just one step at a time."

Liam bit his lip and reached for Theo's hand. With a deep breath, he climbed, his fingers trembling as they gripped the rough surface. When he finally reached the top, Milo cheered. "See? That wasn't so hard!"

Liam smiled weakly. It was hard, but he had done it. He could keep going.

The Hidden Wonder

As they climbed higher, the boys discovered something unexpected—a narrow path leading off the main trail, almost hidden by overgrown bushes. "Let's check it out!" Milo said, his eyes gleaming.

"Are you sure?" Liam asked nervously.

"Come on, it'll be fun!" Theo said, already pushing through the bushes.

The path led to a small clearing with a sheer rock face towering above them. At the base was a tiny cave, just big enough for the boys to crouch inside. "This is so cool!" Milo exclaimed, peeking into the cave.

But Liam barely noticed the cave. His eyes were fixed on the rock face. It wasn't as tall as the peak of Ridge Hill, but it was still intimidating. "You're not going to climb that, are you?" he asked.

Theo grinned. "Why not? It's perfect. And you're coming too."

"No way," Liam said, backing up. "I can't climb that."

"Yes, you can," Milo said. "Look, it's not that steep, and we'll help you."

Liam shook his head. "What if I slip? What if I fall?"

Theo put a hand on Liam's shoulder. "You won't fall. And even if you slip, we'll be right here to catch you. Trust us."

A Leap of Courage

Liam stared at the rock face, his heart racing. He wanted to say no, to turn back and wait for his friends to be done. But something inside him stirred—a small, stubborn voice that said, "You've come this far. Don't give up now."

Taking a deep breath, Liam placed his hands on the rock. The surface was rough but sturdy, and he felt a flicker of hope. "Okay," he whispered. "I'll try."

With Milo guiding him from below and Theo calling encouragement from above, Liam began to climb. His muscles ached, and his hands grew sweaty, but he kept going. When he slipped once, his friends caught him, just as they had promised.

Finally, after what felt like hours, Liam reached the top. He pulled himself over the edge and collapsed, his chest heaving. When he opened his eyes, he gasped.

The view was breathtaking. Below them, the valley stretched like a patchwork quilt of fields, forests, and rivers.

The sun hung low in the sky, painting everything in shades of gold and orange. For a moment, Liam forgot about his fear. All he could feel was awe.

"You did it!" Theo said, clapping him on the back.

"You're braver than you think," Milo added with a grin.

Liam smiled a genuine smile this time. He had done it. He had faced his fear and climbed higher than he ever thought he could.

The Climb Back Down

The journey down was more straightforward, though Liam still moved carefully. When they reached the base of the hill, he turned to look back at the rock face. It still looked tall, but it didn't scare him as much anymore. It looked like something he had conquered.

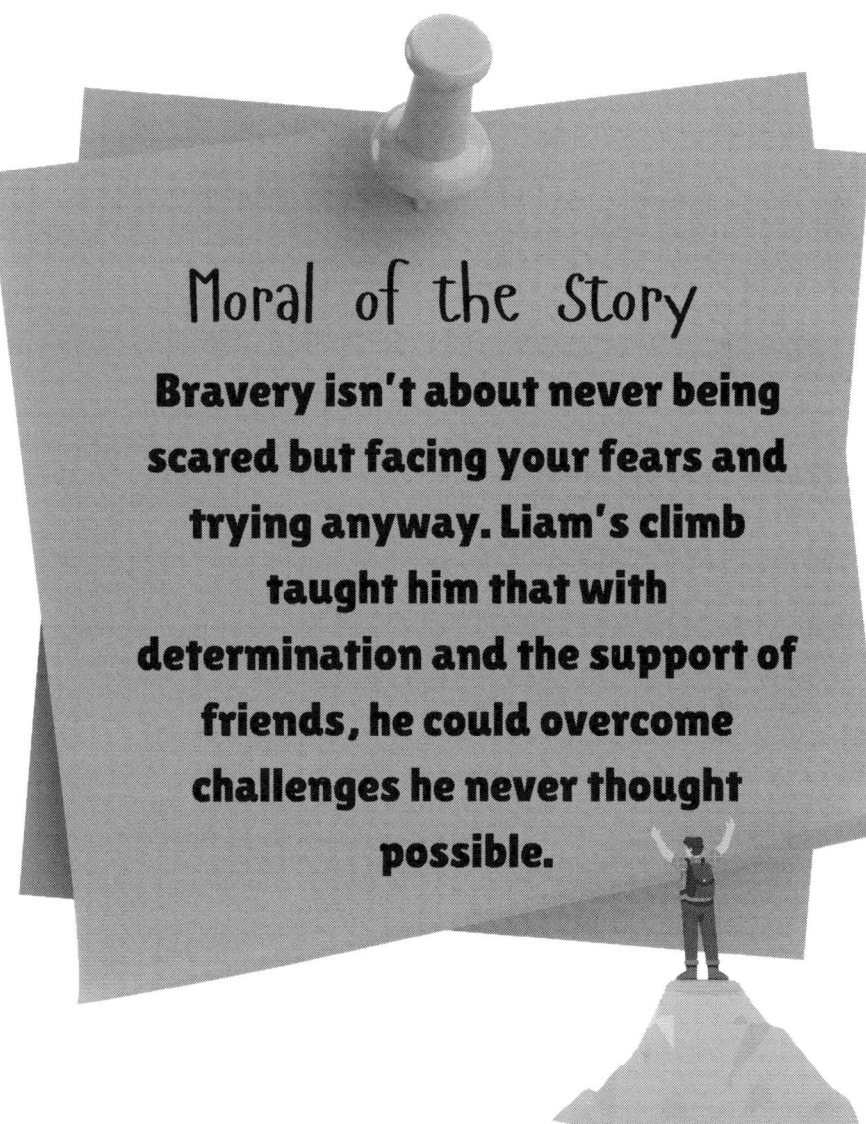

Moral of the Story

Bravery isn't about never being scared but facing your fears and trying anyway. Liam's climb taught him that with determination and the support of friends, he could overcome challenges he never thought possible.

The Library Detective

3

The Library Detective

Max Carter was a boy with a sharp mind and a love for books. Every afternoon, you could find him in the corner of the school library, nose buried in a mystery novel. He loved solving puzzles and imagining himself as a great detective, like the characters in his favorite stories.

But one chilly Monday afternoon, Max noticed something strange. His favorite book, The Case of the Missing Gemstone, was missing from the library shelf. At first, he thought someone had borrowed it, but when he asked Mrs. Harper, the librarian, she frowned.

"That's odd," she said. "Nobody has checked it out."

Max's curiosity sparked. "Could it have been misplaced?" he asked.

Mrs. Harper shook her head. "I don't think so. And it's not just that book. A few others have gone missing too."

Max's heart raced. A mystery right in his school! "Don't worry, Mrs. Harper," he said, straightening his glasses. "Detective Max is on the case."

Gathering Clues

Max pulled out his trusty notebook and began investigating. His first step was to examine the crime scene—the library. He noticed the missing books came from the same section: famous mysteries and adventure stories.

"Someone must really like exciting books," Max muttered, jotting down his first clue.

Next, Max interviewed potential witnesses. He asked his classmates if they had seen anything unusual. Most shook their heads, but his friend Lucas had an interesting observation.

"I saw Benny hanging around the library during recess," Lucas said. "He looked kinda nervous."

Benny was a quiet boy in their class who rarely spoke. Max decided to keep an eye on him.

The Suspect
The next day, Max followed Benny after school. He watched Benny enter the library, glanced around nervously, and slipped a small book into his backpack. Max's heart pounded. He had caught the thief!
But as Max was about to confront Benny, he hesitated. Benny didn't look like someone trying to get away with a crime. He looked... embarrassed.
Curiosity got the better of Max. Instead of stopping Benny, he decided to follow him.

A Surprising Discovery
Max trailed Benny to a quiet corner of the schoolyard, where Benny sat alone on a bench. He took out the book, opened it, and stared at the pages. But instead of reading, Benny just sat there, his face scrunched in frustration.

Max stepped closer, careful not to startle him. "Hey, Benny," he said gently.

Benny jumped, clutching the book. "I didn't mean to—" he stammered.

"It's okay," Max said. "I'm not here to get you in trouble. I want to know why you're taking the books."

Benny hesitated, then sighed. "I wanted to read them, but I... I'm not good at reading. The words are hard, and I don't want anyone to know."

Max felt a pang of sympathy. Benny wasn't stealing for fun; he was struggling and didn't know how to ask for help.

A Plan for Help

"Benny, you don't have to do this alone," Max said. "I can help you learn to read."

"You'd do that?" Benny asked, his eyes wide.

"Of course!" Max said with a smile. "We can meet here every day after school and practice."

Benny nodded slowly, a small smile creeping onto his face. "Thanks, Max."

Building Friendship

Over the next few weeks, Max and Benny worked together. They started with simple books, and Max helped Benny sound out tricky words. At first, it was slow, but Benny's confidence grew with each session.

Max also spoke to Mrs. Harper, who agreed to let Benny borrow books without embarrassment. "Everyone starts somewhere," she said kindly.

Benny's improvement was noticeable. One day, he proudly read a whole page without stumbling. "I did it!" he exclaimed.

"You're doing great," Max said. "Soon, you'll be reading mysteries faster than I can."

Solving the Final Mystery

As Benny's reading improved, Max realized their sessions had solved multiple mysteries. Benny had gained confidence, and Max had gained a new friend.

One afternoon, Mrs. Harper called Max to the library. "Detective Max, you've solved the case of the missing books," she said with a smile. "But you've also brought someone closer to the joy of reading. That's the best kind of mystery to solve."

Max beamed. He had started the investigation to find missing books but found something even better—a way to help someone in need.

Moral of the Story

Curiosity and problem-solving can lead to unexpected discoveries. Max learned that helping others is just as important as solving mysteries, and Benny discovered that asking for help can open the door to new opportunities.

The Art of Being Oliver

4

The Art of Being Oliver

Oliver Blotts was different from your average third-grader. While other kids played soccer or collected trading cards, Oliver spent hours in his backyard, painting everything he could find—rocks, leaves, even the occasional garden gnome. He loved art, but there was one problem: his art was... unusual.

While his classmates painted apples or smiling suns, Oliver painted giraffes wearing roller skates and dolphins playing saxophones. His art was wild, colorful, and bursting with imagination. But it wasn't "normal," which worried Oliver.

"I don't get it," he said one day, frowning at a particularly vibrant portrait of a skateboarding turtle. "Why can't I just paint regular stuff, like everyone else?"

His best friend, Max, shrugged. "Because you're Oliver. And Oliver is... different."

Oliver wasn't sure if that was a compliment or not.

The Contest Announcement

On Monday morning, Mrs. Timmons, the art teacher, walked into class with a stack of flyers. "Attention, artists!" she announced. "The annual school art contest is here! This year's theme is 'Creative Expression.' Show us what makes you unique!"

The class buzzed with excitement. Everyone was eager to participate—everyone except Oliver.

"I'm not entering," Oliver told Max at lunch. "What if they laugh at my art?"

Max raised an eyebrow. "Dude, you painted a flamingo doing karate last week. If they laugh, it's probably because they're jealous they didn't think of it first."

Oliver wasn't convinced. But deep down, a tiny part of him wanted to give it a shot.

The Painting Begins

That weekend, Oliver set up his easel in the backyard. He stared at the blank canvas, his paintbrush hovering in the air. "Something unique," he muttered. "Something that screams 'Oliver.'"

He started with a splash of yellow, then added swirls of blue and splatters of green. Soon, the canvas came alive with colors and shapes. He painted a lion in a polka-dot suit, juggling pineapples while a parade of penguins marched behind it, holding balloons.

"It's weird," Oliver said, stepping back to look at his masterpiece. "But it's me."

Just then, his little sister, Emma, peeked over his shoulder. "That lion looks like Dad in his work suit."

Oliver grinned. "Yeah, but Dad doesn't juggle pineapples. Yet."

The Big Reveal

On the contest day, the gymnasium was transformed into an art gallery. Oliver's stomach churned as he carried his painting inside. The other entries were impressive: realistic landscapes, detailed portraits, and one suspiciously perfect bowl of fruit. Oliver's painting looked like a circus exploded onto the canvas.

Max nudged him. "Relax. Your painting is awesome. Besides, who wants to look at another boring apple?"

Oliver wasn't so sure.

Oliver hid behind a pillar when the judging began, too nervous to watch. He could hear the judges murmuring as they examined each piece. When they reached his painting, there was a long pause.

"Is that a lion juggling pineapples?" one judge asked.

"It's... unique," another said.

Oliver's heart sank. Unique wasn't always a good thing.

The Surprise

Mrs. Timmons stood on the stage with a microphone. "And now, the winner of this year's art contest…"

Oliver braced himself for disappointment.

"…Oliver Blotts!"

"What?!" Oliver's jaw dropped. He stumbled onto the stage, his face as red as a tomato.

"Oliver's painting captures the true spirit of creativity," Mrs. Timmons said, holding up his artwork. "It's imaginative, bold, and wonderfully original. It reminds us that art isn't about fitting in but standing out."

The gym erupted into applause. Oliver spotted Max in the crowd, giving him two thumbs up.

The Lesson

After the contest, kids crowded around Oliver, asking about his painting.

"Why a lion in a suit?" one girl asked.

"Why not?" Oliver replied, grinning.

That night, Oliver hung his winning painting on his bedroom wall. For the first time, he didn't feel embarrassed about being different. He felt proud.

Moral of the Story

Being yourself is the most beautiful thing you can be. Whether it's through art, hobbies, or how you think, your uniqueness makes you special. So don't be afraid to stand out—because standing out makes the world more colorful.

The Kindness Chain

5

The Kindness Chain

Alex Porter was a kid with big ideas and an even bigger imagination. Whether building a rocket ship out of cardboard or trying to train his cat to fetch, Alex always had something up his sleeve. But his latest idea was different. It wasn't about having fun—it was about making the world a little better.

It all started one rainy Wednesday. Alex was at his desk, doodling in his math notebook (which was supposed to be filled with multiplication tables), when he noticed Jonah slouching in the seat next to him. Jonah was the quiet kid in class. He always looked like he had a hundred-pound backpack weighing him down, even when he wasn't wearing one.

"What's up with Jonah?" Alex whispered to his best friend, Charlie.

Charlie shrugged. "Dunno. Maybe he's just having a bad day."

Alex frowned. He hated seeing people sad. That's when an idea popped into his head. A tiny idea. A sticky note-sized idea.

The First Note

Alex grabbed a sticky note from his backpack at recess and scribbled, "You're awesome, and don't let anyone tell you otherwise!" Then, in his best ninja impersonation, he crept over to Jonah's desk and stuck the note inside his math book.

"Mission accomplished," Alex muttered, darting back to his seat.

The next day, Jonah walked into class with a small smile. He sat up a little straighter, too. Alex grinned. One good deed down, he thought.

But what Alex didn't expect was what happened next. At lunchtime, he spotted Jonah leaving a note on Maya's locker. Maya, who had been having a tough week after losing her dog, found the note and lit up like a Christmas tree.

The note read: "You have the kindest heart! Don't stop smiling."

Alex watched, amazed. Jonah had paid the kindness forward. And just like that, the kindness chain was born.

The Chain Reaction

By Friday, the whole school was buzzing with mysterious sticky notes. They popped up in lockers, on water bottles, and even on the principal's coffee cup (which read, "Thanks for keeping us all in line, Principal Higgins! P.S. Love your tie!").

Alex couldn't believe how far his little note had gone. Everywhere he looked, people were smiling, laughing, and high-fiving. Even the janitor, grumpy Mr. Grumbles, whistled while he mopped the hallway.

But then, trouble struck.

The Sticky Note Mystery

On Monday morning, Principal Higgins made an announcement.

"Attention, students! It seems we have a sticky note bandit on the loose. While these notes are very kind, they're also creating a mess. Let's keep our school tidy, okay?"

Alex slumped in his seat. Uh-oh.

"What's wrong?" Charlie whispered.

"I think Principal Higgins is onto me," Alex whispered back.

Charlie raised an eyebrow. "You're the sticky note bandit?"

"Well, I started it... kind of," Alex admitted. "But now it's out of control!"

Charlie smirked. "Dude, you created a kindness monster."

Alex groaned. "A kindness chain, not a monster."

Still, he couldn't help but worry. What if Principal Higgins shut down the whole thing? What if people stopped spreading kindness?

A Kindness Emergency

Alex called an emergency meeting at recess in the treehouse behind his house. Charlie, Max, and their other friend Sam squeezed into the tiny space, where Alex explained his dilemma.

"We have to save the kindness chain," Alex declared. "But how?"

"Why don't we tell people to stop leaving sticky notes everywhere?" Max suggested.

"But that's how the chain works!" Alex protested.

"What if we go bigger?" Charlie said. "Like, instead of notes, we do something huge to spread kindness."

Alex's eyes lit up. "Like what?"

"I don't know yet," Charlie admitted. "But it's gotta be epic."

The Big Kindness Plan

The boys brainstormed all afternoon. Finally, they came up with the perfect plan: a Kindness Fair. It would be a school-wide event where everyone could share acts of kindness. They'd set up a kindness wall where people could leave positive messages, a station for making friendship bracelets, and even a cookie booth with complimentary treats.

"We'll call it 'The Great Kindness Fair,'" Alex announced. "And we'll invite the whole school!"

The next day, the boys pitched their idea to Principal Higgins. At first, the principal looked skeptical.

"Kindness is important," he said, stroking his tie. "But how will you keep things organized?"
"We'll handle everything!" Alex promised. "No sticky notes, no mess—just kindness."
Principal Higgins thought for a moment, then smiled. "All right. Let's give it a try."

The Kindness Fair
The following week, the school gym was transformed into a kindness wonderland. There were kindness stations everywhere: one for writing thank-you notes, another for making handmade cards, and even a "compliment corner" where kids could exchange kind words.

Alex was in charge of the kindness wall, which quickly filled up with messages like:
- "You're the best teacher ever, Mrs. Timmons!"
- "Thanks for sharing your lunch, Max!"
- "To the person who helped me with my math homework: You're a genius!"

By the end of the day, the gym was bursting with positivity. Kids were laughing, teachers were smiling, and Principal Higgins even joined the compliment corner.

"This is amazing," Alex said, watching the chaos with a grin.

"See?" Charlie said. "Bigger is better."

The Chain Continues

After the Kindness Fair, the sticky notes didn't stop entirely but became part of something bigger. The kindness chain lived on—not just in notes, but in high-fives, thank-yous, and small acts of kindness that spread throughout the school.

One afternoon, Alex found a note in his locker. It read: "Thanks for starting the kindness chain. You're awesome!"

Alex smiled. He didn't know who wrote it, but he felt warm inside. He didn't need credit or recognition. Knowing he'd made a difference was enough.

Moral of the Story

Kindness is contagious. A small act of kindness can grow into something much bigger, creating a ripple effect that touches everyone around you. So be brave, take the first step, and pay it forward—you never know how far your kindness will go.

The Forest Guardians

6

The Forest Guardians

Ben and Ryan Parker weren't your typical 9-year-old twins. They didn't just share the same spiky haircut and freckled faces—they also shared a knack for finding trouble wherever they went. Whether it was climbing the tallest trees or daring each other to eat the weirdest bugs (spoiler: Ryan once ate an ant), they were always up to something.

So, when their parents announced a family camping trip to Pinewood Forest, the twins were thrilled.

"A whole weekend in the woods?" Ben exclaimed. "We can be explorers!"

"Or treasure hunters!" Ryan added.

"Or professional bug catchers!"

"Let's not catch bugs," their mom said, wrinkling her nose. "Just... try not to cause chaos, okay?"

Ben and Ryan exchanged a mischievous grin. "Chaos? Us? Never."

The Trouble in the Woods

On the first morning of their trip, the twins bolted out of the tent with their backpacks and binoculars, ready for adventure. They tromped through the forest, laughing as they pretended to be secret agents on a mission to find hidden treasure.

"Agent Ben, do you see that suspicious bush?" Ryan whispered dramatically.

Ben peered through his binoculars. "It's just a bush, Agent Ryan. But that rock over there? Super suspicious."

As they approached the "suspicious" rock, Ryan froze. "Wait… what's that smell?"

It didn't take long to find the source: a pile of litter—empty soda cans, crumpled chip bags, and even a soggy shoe—spilled across the ground.

"Gross!" Ben said, poking a can with a stick. "Who leaves their junk in the forest?"

Ryan frowned. "Not cool. Animals live here! What if they think this stuff is food?"

As if on cue, a squirrel scurried by, dragging a candy wrapper like a prized acorn. The twins watched in horror as it tried to nibble the shiny plastic.

"No way!" Ryan yelled, shooing the squirrel away. "This forest needs help."

Ben nodded, a determined look on his face. "It's up to us, Agent Ryan. We're on a new mission: Operation Clean-Up."

Recruiting the Team

At the campsite, Ben and Ryan rallied their friends, Mia and Jake, who were camping nearby with their families.

"Let me get this straight," Mia said, crossing her arms. "You want us to spend our day cleaning up other people's trash?"

"Exactly!" Ben said. "Think of it like being superheroes, but for the forest!"

Jake scratched his head. "Do we get capes?"

"No, but you might find treasure," Ryan said, wiggling his eyebrows. "Like… I dunno… an old pirate coin."

"Or more soggy shoes," Mia muttered.

But eventually, they agreed. Armed with gloves, trash bags, and determination, the four friends set off to clean up the forest.

The Great Forest Clean-Up

The clean-up started smoothly. Mia found a discarded water bottle near a tree, Jake picked up a rusty tin can, and Ryan pried an old frisbee out of a bush.

"This is easy," Ben said, tossing a crumpled juice box into his bag. "We'll have this place spotless in no time."

But then they reached the creek. The sight made them gasp.

"Holy guacamole," Ryan whispered.

The water was littered with everything from plastic bags to an actual shopping cart (how it got there, no one knew). A raccoon perched on the edge of the creek, poking at a floating candy bar wrapper like it was deciding whether to eat it.

"This is a disaster," Mia said. "We'll need more help."

"Let's call the parents," Jake suggested.
Ben shook his head. "No way. We started this mission, and we're going to finish it. We need a plan."

Ryan's Genius Idea
Ryan's eyes lit up. "What if we make it a competition? People love competitions!"
Ben raised an eyebrow. "What kind of competition?"
Ryan grinned. "A trash-collecting contest! Whoever picks up the most trash wins… uh… bragging rights?"
"And maybe some s'mores," Mia added.
"Deal!" Jake said. "Let's do it."

The Contest Begins
The kids ran back to the main campground and spread the word. Soon, a small army of campers—parents, siblings, and even the grumpy park ranger—joined.
"Remember," Ryan announced, standing on a tree stump like a general. "Every piece of trash you pick up is one point. Bonus points for weird stuff!"

"What counts as weird?" asked a little boy holding a plastic fork.

"Keep looking," Ben said with a grin.

The forest erupted into activity. People fanned out, picking up everything from soda cans to stray flip-flops. Jake found an old rubber duck, Mia discovered a bicycle tire, and one of the parents triumphantly held up a bent metal spoon.

Meanwhile, Ben and Ryan worked as a team, clearing the creek of plastic bags and pulling the mysterious shopping cart out of the water.

"Bonus points for the cart!" Ben cheered.

"Double bonus points for not falling in!" Ryan added.

The Celebration

By the end of the day, the campers had collected dozens of trash bags. The forest looked clean and beautiful again, and the animals—especially the squirrel—seemed much happier.

The park ranger, who rarely smiled, gave the twins a nod of approval. "Good work, kids. You should be proud."

"We are," Ryan said, wiping mud off his face. "Also very, very tired."

That night, the twins and their friends sat around the campfire, roasting marshmallows and telling stories about their "heroic" clean-up mission.

"I still think we should've gotten capes," Jake said, munching on a s'more.

Ben grinned. "Maybe next time. Because the Forest Guardians aren't done yet."

"Guardians?" Mia asked, raising an eyebrow.

"Yeah," Ben said. "That's us. We're like superheroes, but for the forest!"

Ryan nodded. "And every superhero needs a cool name."

"Do they also need to smell like garbage?" Mia teased, wrinkling her nose.

The twins laughed. "That's just part of the job."

Moral of the Story

Caring for the environment isn't just about picking up trash—it's about taking responsibility for the world we live in. When you see a problem, don't wait for someone else to fix it. Be a leader, take action, and inspire others to do the same because even small efforts can make a big difference!

The Brave New Friend

7

The Brave New Friend

Lucas Wilkins had a simple philosophy in life: if it didn't involve dragons, pizza, or video games, it probably wasn't worth his time. But even Lucas couldn't ignore the buzz in his fourth-grade class one Monday morning.

"There's a new kid!" Max whispered as Lucas slid into his seat. "His name's Raj. He's from... somewhere far away."

"Like Australia?" Lucas asked, imagining kangaroos hopping down the hall.

"Farther," Max said, wide-eyed. "And he talks funny."

Lucas raised an eyebrow. He didn't know what Max meant by "talks funny," but he didn't have time to figure it out because Mrs. Palmer clapped her hands.

"Class, meet Raj Kumar!" she announced.

A small boy shuffled into the room. He had dark, neatly combed hair, wore a bright yellow shirt, and clutched a lunchbox decorated with elephants.

"Elephants are cool," Lucas thought.

But the rest of the class wasn't as kind.

"Why's he wearing a yellow shirt?" whispered Liam from the back. "Is it summer in his country or something?"

Lucas frowned. So what if he's different? But he didn't say anything.

Lunchroom Loner

By lunchtime, Lucas had mostly forgotten about Raj—until he saw him sitting alone in the corner of the cafeteria, poking at a mysterious green blob in his lunchbox. The rest of the kids were crowded around Max, who was demonstrating his ability to fit an entire slice of pizza in his mouth.

Lucas turned back to Raj. He looked... lonely.

"Should we invite him over?" Lucas asked Max.

"Raj? Nah," Max said, his mouth full of pizza. "He's probably fine."

But Lucas wasn't so sure.

The First Encounter

The next day, Lucas made up his mind. He grabbed his tray and plopped down at Raj's table.

"Hey," Lucas said.

Raj looked up, startled. "Oh. Hello."

Lucas glanced at Raj's lunch. The green blob was back, now accompanied by a stack of flatbread.

"What's that?" Lucas asked, pointing to the blob.

"It's saag paneer," Raj said. "It's spinach and cheese."

Lucas wrinkled his nose. "Spinach and cheese? Together?"

Raj grinned. "It's perfect. Want to try?"

Lucas hesitated. He wasn't sure about this whole spinach-cheese combo, but Raj looked hopeful.

"Sure," Lucas said. He took a tiny bite. To his surprise, it wasn't terrible. It was... good.

"Not bad," Lucas admitted. "Do you eat this every day?"

Raj laughed. "No! Sometimes we have dosa, or biryani, or—"

"Hold up," Lucas interrupted. "What's a dosa?"

Raj's eyes lit up as he explained. "It's like a pancake, but crispy, and you dip it in chutney or sambal."

Lucas grinned. "Sounds awesome. Way better than cafeteria pizza."

Cultural Exchange

Over the next few days, Lucas and Raj became friends. Raj taught Lucas to say a few words in Hindi (although Lucas's pronunciation made Raj laugh so hard that he almost cried). Lucas, in turn, introduced Raj to the wonders of pepperoni pizza and the school's best hide-and-seek spots.

One day during recess, Raj brought a cricket bat to school.

"Is that for whacking home runs?" Lucas asked.

Raj chuckled. "No, it's for cricket. It's like baseball, but different. Want to try?"

Lucas wasn't sure he'd ever figure out the rules of cricket, but swinging the bat and trying to hit the ball was more fun than he expected. Soon, half the class had gathered to watch—or join in.

"Hey, this is cool," Max said, stepping up to bat.

Raj smiled. "Thanks."

The Talent Show Plan

One afternoon, Mrs. Palmer announced a school talent show.

"We need volunteers to share something special with the class," she said. "It could be a song, a dance, a skill, or something from your culture."

Lucas immediately turned to Raj. "You should do cricket!"

Raj hesitated. "I don't know... What if they laugh at me?"

"They won't," Lucas said. "And if they do, I'll throw pizza at them."

Raj laughed, but he still looked nervous.

"Come on," Lucas said. "You showed me your culture. Now, show everyone else. I'll help."

The Big Day
When talent show day arrived, Raj and Lucas stood backstage, waiting for their turn.
"What if I mess up?" Raj whispered.
"You won't," Lucas said. "And if you do, I'll distract them by doing the worm."
Raj laughed. "Promise?"
"Promise."
When it was their turn, Raj stepped onto the stage, holding his cricket bat. Lucas followed with a bucket of tennis balls.
"Hi," Raj began. His voice shook a little, but he kept going. "I'm Raj, and I will show you how to play cricket."
He explained the basics of the game while Lucas demonstrated (poorly) how to bowl and bat. The audience laughed—not at Raj, but at Lucas's exaggerated stumbles and dramatic misses.
"Whoa!" Lucas yelled as he pretended to trip over the bat.

By the end of the demonstration, the whole class was cheering.

A New Perspective

After the show, Raj was surrounded by classmates asking questions.

"Where'd you learn to play cricket?" asked Mia.

"Can we play at recess?" added Jake.

Raj beamed. "Sure!"

As Lucas watched Raj chat with their classmates, he felt a warm glow in his chest. Raj wasn't "the new kid" anymore. He was just... Raj.

The Lesson

The next day at lunch, Raj sat with Lucas and the rest of the group. This time, nobody teased him about his accent or his lunchbox. Mia even tried a bite of saag paneer.

"This is good," she said, looking surprised.

"Told you," Lucas said with a grin.

From then on, things were different. Raj wasn't just included—he was celebrated. And Lucas learned something important: sometimes, all it takes is one brave step to turn a stranger into a friend.

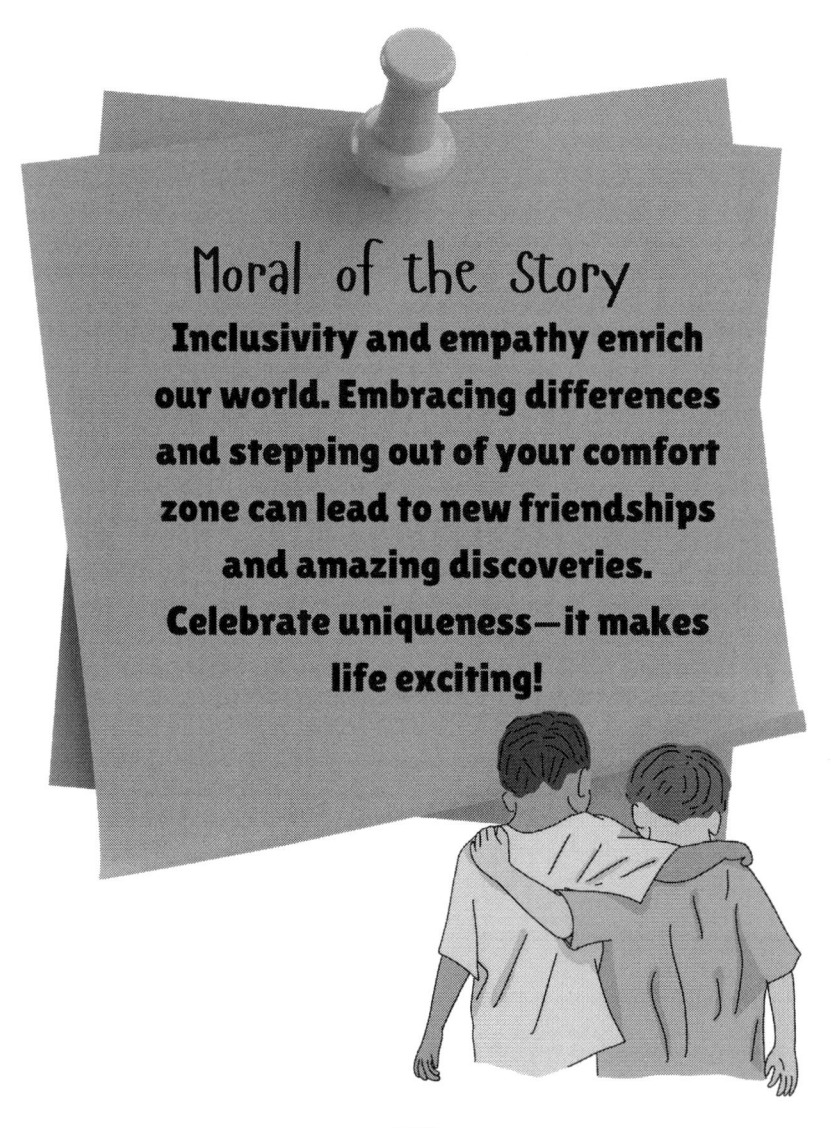

Moral of the Story

Inclusivity and empathy enrich our world. Embracing differences and stepping out of your comfort zone can lead to new friendships and amazing discoveries. Celebrate uniqueness—it makes life exciting!

The Magic of Saying Sorry

8

The Magic of Saying Sorry

Ethan, was the exact opposite. Ethan was calm, careful, and, most importantly, loved his toys more than anything else.

Ethan's favorite toy was a shiny, red remote-control race car named Turbo. Turbo wasn't just any toy. Ethan had saved up every penny of his allowance to buy it and treated the car like a treasure. Sam, however, secretly thought it looked like just another boring car. That is, until one rainy afternoon when boredom took over.

An Accident Waiting to Happen

"Mom, there's nothing to do!" Sam groaned, flopping onto the couch. Outside, rain pelted against the windows, canceling his plans to play basketball with his friends.

"Well, why don't you find something fun to do with Ethan?" Mom called from the kitchen.

"Ethan's just sitting there polishing that car again," Sam muttered. But an idea struck him as he peeked into Ethan's room and saw Turbo gleaming on the desk.

It started innocently enough. "Hey, Ethan," Sam said casually, "can I try Turbo? Just once? I'll be super careful."

Ethan hesitated, hugging Turbo protectively. "You have to promise not to crash it," he said, narrowing his eyes.

"Pfft, I'm an amazing driver," Sam said, puffing out his chest. "I promise."

That promise lasted all of two minutes. Sam zoomed Turbo down the hallway like a professional racer, complete with sound effects: "Vroom! Beep beep! Watch out, pedestrians!" But when he tried a daring 180-degree spin, Turbo skidded right into the corner of the wall with a loud CRUNCH.

Sam froze, staring at the front wheel dangling from its socket.

"Oh no," he whispered. "This is bad. This is really, really bad."

The Great Cover-Up

Sam's first thought was to tell Ethan the truth. But then he imagined Ethan's wide eyes filling with tears, his voice trembling as he said, "You broke Turbo?!" The thought was unbearable.

So, naturally, Sam did the next best thing: he grabbed a roll of tape from the junk drawer and tried to fix it. He taped the wheel back on (crookedly), wiped off the scratches with his sleeve, and carefully placed Turbo back on Ethan's desk. It wasn't perfect, but maybe Ethan wouldn't notice… right?

The Truth Comes Out

Ethan noticed.

That evening, Ethan ran into the living room holding Turbo. "Sam!" he cried, his voice a mix of anger and heartbreak. "Turbo's broken!"

Sam tried to act surprised. "What? No way! Are you sure? Maybe it came like that…"

Ethan glared. "Turbo didn't come with a crooked wheel and tape all over it. What happened?"

Sam shuffled his feet, guilt twisting in his stomach. "Uh, maybe it, uh, got bumped?"

"Bumped? BUMPED?" Ethan's face turned red. "You did this, didn't you?"

Sam opened his mouth to deny it but stopped. He couldn't lie to Ethan anymore. "Okay, fine," he admitted. "I broke it. But it was an accident! I didn't mean to!"

"You PROMISED," Ethan said, his voice cracking. He turned and stomped out of the room, clutching Turbo like a wounded soldier.

The Apology Plan

Sam spent the rest of the evening feeling awful. He tried distracting himself with video games, but the image of Ethan's teary eyes kept popping into his head.

Finally, Mom poked her head into his room. "What's wrong, Sam? You've been unusually quiet."

Sam sighed. "I broke Ethan's car and tried to cover it up. Now he hates me."

Mom sat on the bed beside him. "He doesn't hate you, Sam. He's just upset because Turbo is important to him. But you know what might help?"

"What?"

"A real apology," Mom said with a smile. "Saying sorry shows you care, and it can fix more than just toys."

Sam nodded slowly. "But what if he doesn't forgive me?"

"Sometimes," Mom said, "it takes courage to do the right thing."

Operation Fix Turbo

The following day, Sam found Ethan sitting on the porch with Turbo in his lap in the backyard. Sam walked up slowly, holding a small toolbox.

"Hey, Ethan," he said, scratching the back of his neck. "Can I sit?"

Ethan shrugged. "Whatever."

Sam sat down and took a deep breath. "I'm really sorry, Ethan. I shouldn't have taken Turbo without being more careful and shouldn't have tried to cover it up. That was wrong."

Ethan didn't say anything but didn't tell Sam to leave either.

"I brought my toolbox," Sam continued. "I think we can fix Turbo together. You're way better at details, and I can handle the hard stuff."

Ethan glanced at the toolbox, then at Sam. "You really think we can fix it?"

"Totally," Sam said with a grin. "Turbo's tough. He just needs a little TLC."

Ethan sighed, but a small smile crept onto his face. "Okay. Let's try."

Turbo's Comeback

The two brothers spent the next hour tinkering with Turbo. Sam carefully unscrewed the broken wheel while Ethan cleaned the scratches. They laughed when Sam accidentally dropped a screw into the grass and had to crawl around looking for it.

By the time they were done, Turbo looked as good as new—maybe even better. "You did a great job on the paint touch-up," Sam said. "Turbo's practically glowing."

Ethan beamed. "And you got the wheel back on perfectly. Thanks, Sam."

A New Tradition

Ethan and Sam took Turbo for a victory lap around the driveway that afternoon. They cheered every time Turbo made a flawless turn, and Ethan even let Sam drive (under close supervision).

Later, Ethan turned to Sam. "You know, you're pretty good at fixing stuff. Maybe we should try building something together next time."

Sam grinned. "Yeah? How about a robot?"

Ethan's eyes lit up. "A robot that can drive Turbo!"

And just like that, the Parker brothers started a new tradition: building and fixing things together.

Moral of the Story

Apologizing takes courage but leads to stronger relationships.

SORRY

The Time Keeper

9

The Time Keeper

Eli Bennett was a great kid, but if there was one thing he could have improved at, it was time management. He was always late—late for school, late for soccer practice, and, much to his mom's frustration, even late for dinner. If you asked Eli, he'd say, "I don't mean to be late—it just… happens!"

His best friend, Jake, was the total opposite. Jake was always on time, organized, and reminded Eli of their plans. "Eli, you've got to get it together," Jake said one day after waiting ten minutes for Eli to show up at the park. "You can't keep leaving people hanging!"

Eli shrugged. "Relax, Jake. I'll work on it."

The Birthday Disaster

A few weeks later, Jake had a big birthday party planned. "It's going to be awesome!" Jake said, handing Eli an invitation. "Don't be late, okay? The party starts at two, and I have a surprise for everyone."

"Two o'clock. Got it!" Eli promised.

But on the day of the party, Eli got distracted. He started building a Lego spaceship and then decided to draw a comic about it, and before he knew it, his mom poked her head into his room.

"Eli, aren't you supposed to be somewhere?"

Eli glanced at the clock. "Oh no! Jake's party!" It was already 3:30.

He raced to Jake's house, but the party was over by the time he got there. Jake was outside, helping his parents clean up. When he saw Eli, his face fell. "You missed it," Jake said quietly. "We had cake, games, and even a magician. I was hoping you'd be there."

"I'm so sorry, Jake," Eli said, his heart sinking. "I lost track of time."

Jake shook his head. "You always lose track of time. It's not just about being late—it's about keeping your promises."

Those words stung, but Eli knew Jake was right.

The Plan to Change

That night, Eli sat on his bed, thinking about how he'd let Jake down. He didn't want to be the kid who was always late or who couldn't be counted on. "I've got to fix this," he said to himself.

The following day, he told his mom everything. "I need to get better at being on time," Eli admitted. "But I don't know how."

His mom smiled and handed him an old watch. "This belonged to your grandpa," she said. "He was the most reliable person I've ever known. Maybe this will help you keep track of time."

Eli slipped the watch onto his wrist. It was a little big, but he liked the way it ticked. It felt like a fresh start.

Practice Makes Perfect

Eli decided to treat being on time like a game. He set alarms on his watch and challenged himself to beat them. "Five minutes to get dressed—go!" he'd shout, racing to pull on his clothes. "Seven minutes to brush my teeth and pack my bag—ready, set, go!"

At first, it was hard. He still slipped up occasionally, like forgetting his library books and running back for them. But over time, Eli started getting better. He showed up to soccer practice early. He got to the bus stop with time to spare. Even his teacher, Mrs. Carter, noticed the change.

"Great job, Eli," she said one morning when he was the first to turn in his homework. "You're really stepping up."

The Class Party Idea

One day, Mrs. Carter mentioned that her birthday was coming up. "I don't usually make a big deal out of it," she said, "but I'll be turning 40, so I guess that's special."

Eli's class decided to throw her a surprise party. "We'll need to decorate the classroom, bake a cake, and make sure she doesn't suspect a thing," Jake said, taking charge. Then he looked at Eli. "Eli, think you can help me organize everything?"

Eli's eyes widened. "Me? Organize?"

"You've been super reliable lately," Jake said. "I think you'd do a great job."

Eli felt a swell of pride. "I'm in."

Party Planning Like a Pro

Over the next week, Eli used his trusty watch to plan everything. He set reminders for when to buy decorations, practice their surprise song, and bake the cake. He even helped Jake distract Mrs. Carter during lunch so the rest of the class could set up.

Everything went perfectly on the day of the party. When Mrs. Carter entered the classroom and saw the balloons, streamers, and cake, she gasped. "You did all this for me?" she asked, tears in her eyes.

"Happy birthday, Mrs. Carter!" the class shouted.

Eli led the group in singing "Happy Birthday," and Mrs. Carter hugged him. "Thank you, Eli," she said. "You've become a leader."

A New Reputation

From that day on, Eli wasn't known as the kid who was always late. He was the kid who could be counted on to show up, keep promises, and help others. And even though the watch had helped, Eli knew his determination had made the biggest difference.

One afternoon, Jake handed Eli a new invitation. "This time, it's just us hanging out at the park," Jake said with a grin. Do you think you can make it on time?"

Eli smiled, tapping his watch. "I'll be there five minutes early."

Moral of the Story

Taking responsibility for your actions helps you grow into a trusted and dependable leader. Eli learned that being on time wasn't just about clocks—it was about showing others they mattered.

The Brave Listener

10

The Brave Listener

Lucas Jackson was the kind of kid who could make anyone laugh. Lucas always found a way to brighten someone's day, whether with his spot-on impressions of their teacher, Mr. Miller, or his goofy dance moves during recess. That's why it puzzled him when his friend Jonah stopped smiling.

Jonah was usually cheerful and full of energy. He'd been the fastest runner in their last school race and always had the best jokes. But lately, Jonah seemed distant. He sat quietly during lunch, picked at his food, and hardly spoke during soccer practice.

"What's up with Jonah?" Lucas asked his friend Max one day.

Max shrugged. "Dunno. Maybe he's just tired."

But Lucas wasn't convinced. He had a feeling something bigger was bothering Jonah.

Taking the First Step

The next day at lunch, Lucas decided to sit next to Jonah. He noticed that Jonah had barely touched his peanut butter sandwich, a sure sign something was wrong. Jonah loved peanut butter sandwiches.

"Hey, Jonah," Lucas said, nudging him gently. "You've been super quiet lately. Is everything okay?"

Jonah shrugged, not meeting Lucas's eyes. "I'm fine."

Lucas tilted his head. "You don't seem fine. You can talk to me, you know. Whatever it is, I'll listen."

For a moment, Jonah didn't say anything. Then, in a small voice, he muttered, "It's my dad."

Lucas leaned closer. "What about your dad?"

Jonah hesitated, then finally said, "He might lose his job. My mom's been worried, and my dad's been upset all the time. They think I don't notice, but I do."

Lucas's heart sank. He didn't know much about jobs, but he could tell this was serious. "Wow. That sounds really tough," he said softly. "I'm sorry, Jonah."

Jonah nodded, his eyes fixed on his lunch tray. "I just don't know what to do. I can't fix it."

Finding a Way to Help

After school, Lucas couldn't stop thinking about Jonah's problem. He wanted to help, but how? He couldn't make Jonah's dad's job problems go away, but maybe he could do something to make things a little easier for Jonah.

The following day, Lucas had an idea. During recess, he found Jonah sitting by himself near the swings. "Hey, Jonah," he said, plopping down beside him. "I've been thinking. We can't fix everything, but maybe we can do something to cheer up your dad."

Jonah looked skeptical. "Like what?"

Lucas grinned. "Like Operation Cheer-Up. We could write him a funny card or make him a snack. My mom always says small things can make a big difference."

Jonah thought for a moment, then a small smile crept onto his face. "Okay. Let's try it."

Operation Cheer-Up

The boys went to Lucas's house to start their mission that afternoon. Lucas pulled out a stack of paper and markers. "Let's make a card first," he suggested. "What's something your dad likes?"

Jonah's face lit up. "He loves football. And he's always telling terrible dad jokes."

"Perfect," Lucas said. "We'll draw him as a football player and fill the card with jokes."

The two boys got to work, laughing as they came up with silly drawings and puns. The front of the card showed Jonah's dad wearing a football jersey with the words "#1 Dad" on it. Inside, they wrote jokes like, "Why did the football coach go to the bank? To get his quarterback!"

When they were done, Jonah held up the card, beaming. "He's going to love this."

The Cookie Caper

For their next mission, Lucas suggested baking cookies. "Everyone loves cookies," he said. "They're like happiness you can eat."

Jonah nodded eagerly. "My dad's favorite is oatmeal raisin."

The boys raided Lucas's kitchen, with Jonah mixing the dough and Lucas shaping the cookies. They ended up with a few lopsided ones (and a kitchen covered in flour), but the smell of freshly baked cookies made it all worth it.

Lucas packed the cookies into a small box and tied it with a ribbon as the cookies cooled. "This is officially the Cheer-Up Cookie Kit," he declared.

Delivering the Surprise

That evening, Jonah brought the card and cookies home to his dad. Lucas waited anxiously the next day to hear how it went.

When Jonah walked into school that morning, he was smiling for the first time in days. "Lucas!" he called, running up to him. "It worked! My dad loved the card and the cookies. He laughed so hard at the jokes and even shared the cookies with my mom and me."

Lucas grinned. "That's awesome! How's he doing now?"

Jonah's smile softened. "He's still worried about his job, but last night was the first time I saw him laugh. Thanks, Lucas."

"Hey, you did most of the work," Lucas said, clapping Jonah on the back. "I just helped a little."

A Bigger Lesson

Over the next few weeks, Lucas noticed that Jonah seemed happier. He still had tough days, but he knew he wasn't alone. The boys even started brainstorming other ways to help, like doing extra chores around Jonah's house to take some pressure off his parents.

One afternoon, Jonah turned to Lucas and said, "I thought I had to fix everything by myself. But just having someone to talk to makes it easier."

Lucas nodded. "Yeah. Sometimes just listening is enough."

Moral of the Story

Empathy can turn tough times into opportunities for connection.

The Team Switcher

11

The Team Switcher

Elijah "Eli" Thompson was known as the star player on the Maplewood Elementary basketball team, the Thunderbolts. With his quick moves, sharp passes, and knack for scoring, Eli had led his team to win every friendly game they'd played that year. His classmates cheered him on, and his teammates high-fived him after every match. Eli loved basketball, and he loved being the hero.

But lately, something had been bothering him. During practices, he noticed that his teammates weren't playing together as much as they used to. Players like Jake and Ryan, who were just as skilled as Eli, would hog the ball, ignoring open teammates. Meanwhile, players like Oliver and Malik, who weren't as confident, barely got a chance to touch the ball.

"It's not fair," Eli thought as he watched Oliver awkwardly shuffle around during practice. "Everyone's supposed to play, not just the stars."

A Friendly Match with a Twist
One Friday afternoon, Coach Carter announced an exciting event. "We're having a friendly game against the Oakwood Eagles next week. It's not about winning—this game is about having fun and showing good sportsmanship."

Eli and the rest of the team nodded, but he wasn't sure everyone had heard the part about "good sportsmanship." Jake elbowed Ryan, grinning. "Easy win," he whispered loudly.

"Yeah," Ryan smirked. "We'll crush them."

Eli frowned. Winning was great, but he couldn't shake the feeling that the Thunderbolts weren't a team anymore.

Game Day

The big day arrived, and the Thunderbolts faced off against the Oakwood Eagles in the school gym. The Eagles were known for their enthusiasm but weren't nearly as skilled as the Thunderbolts. Before the game even started, Jake snickered. "This is going to be a joke."

As the first quarter began, the Thunderbolts dominated. Jake and Ryan dribbled circles around the Eagles, scoring easily. But instead of passing to open teammates like Oliver and Malik, they kept the ball between themselves and Eli.

"Eli, over here!" Malik called, waving his arms as he stood open near the hoop.

Eli hesitated. He could pass to Malik, but Jake had already darted toward the hoop. Eli sighed and passed to Jake, who scored another point. The crowd cheered, but Eli didn't feel proud.

By halftime, the Thunderbolts were leading 24-8, but Eli wasn't enjoying the game. He looked at the Eagles, who were struggling but still giving their all. Then he glanced at Oliver and Malik, sitting quietly on the bench.

"This isn't fun," Eli muttered to himself. "It's just... unfair."

The Switch

During the halftime break, an idea popped into Eli's head. It was a little crazy, and he wasn't sure how it would go, but he knew he had to try.

"Coach," Eli said, jogging over to the Eagles' bench. "I think I should play for the Eagles in the second half."

Coach Carter raised an eyebrow. "What's this about, Eli?"

"Well, um…" Eli hesitated, then took a deep breath. "The Thunderbolts are good, but we're not giving the Eagles a fair chance. And honestly, my team's not sharing the ball enough. If I play for the Eagles, it'll be more balanced—and more fun for everyone."

Coach Carter studied Eli for a moment, then smiled. "All right, Eli. If the Eagles are okay with it, you've got my permission."

Eli turned to the Eagles. "What do you guys think? Can I join your team?"

The Eagles' eyes lit up. "Really?" said Dylan, their captain. "You'd do that?"

"Sure," Eli said, grinning. "Let's even things out a bit."

The Comeback

The second half began, and Eli now wore an Eagles jersey. The Thunderbolts looked confused as he jogged onto the court with his new teammates.

"What are you doing, Eli?" Jake hissed.

"Trying something new," Eli said with a shrug.

From the start, the game felt different. Eli didn't just play to score—he played to help the Eagles shine. He passed the ball to Dylan, who surprised everyone with a perfect shot.

He encouraged Daniel, the Eagles' most minor player, to take a risky dribble, which led to another basket. And when Malik tried to block Eli's shot, Eli purposely passed to another Eagle, who scored instead.

The crowd roared. The Eagles were catching up, and the gym buzzed with excitement. Even Oliver, watching from the Thunderbolts' bench, started cheering.

A Game to Remember

By the final quarter, the score was tied 30-30. The Thunderbolts had started passing more, realizing teamwork was the only way to stay ahead. Jake and Ryan shared the ball with Oliver and Malik, who played better with every pass they received.

With thirty seconds left, Eli had the ball. He could take the final shot, but instead, he passed to Daniel, who scored the game-tying basket just as the buzzer rang.

The crowd leaped to their feet, cheering. "What a game!" Coach Carter called. "This is what basketball is all about!"

A Lesson in Sportsmanship

After the game, Jake and Ryan approached Eli. "That was... different," Jake admitted, rubbing the back of his neck. "But it was fun. We should, uh, pass more, huh?"

"Yeah," Ryan said. "You were right, Eli. It's better when everyone gets a chance."

Eli grinned. "Told you."

As the teams shook hands, Dylan turned to Eli. "Thanks for playing with us, Eli. You didn't have to do that, but it made a huge difference."

"Teamwork makes the dream work," Eli said with a laugh.

Moral of the Story

True sportsmanship is about lifting others and playing as a team.

The Music Maker

12

The Music Maker

Herald Parker wasn't like most kids in his school. While other kids loved playing sports, running around the playground, or swapping jokes at lunch, Herald's favorite place was the music room. It wasn't that he didn't like his classmates—he did—but there was something about music that felt magical to him. Music made Herald feel alive, whether it was the sweet notes of a piano or the steady beat of a drum.

But there was one problem: Herald was too shy to let anyone hear him play. Even though he was great at coming up with his tunes on the piano, the thought of performing in front of others made his hands sweat.

"You've got talent, Herald," his music teacher, Mrs. Lacey, often said. "Don't hide it!"

Herald just smiled nervously. "Maybe someday," he'd mumble, though he wasn't sure if that day would ever come.

A Hidden Treasure

One rainy afternoon, Herald stayed inside during recess. With no one around, he wandered into the school's storage room, hoping to find a quiet spot to doodle in his notebook. The storage room was cluttered with old chairs, dusty boxes, and random equipment nobody seemed to use anymore.

As he explored, something caught his eye: a strange, old keyboard tucked away under a pile of blankets. It looked ancient, with faded keys and a few chipped edges. Herald brushed off the dust and pressed a key experimentally.

To his surprise, the keyboard lit up! A soft blue glow shimmered from the key he had pressed, and a sweet note echoed in the room. Herald's eyes widened. He pressed another key, and this time, a green light glowed, accompanied by a cheerful, higher-pitched sound.

"What kind of keyboard is this?" Herald whispered to himself, fascinated.

Excited, he sat down and began experimenting. Every key he pressed lit up in a different color, creating a dazzling display. The more he played, the brighter and more colorful the lights became, as if the keyboard encouraged him.

"This is amazing," Herald thought, a grin spreading across his face.

A Secret Melody

From that day on, Herald spent every free moment in the storage room with the magical keyboard. He composed little melodies, blending the glowing colors with his music. The lights inspired him to try new things, and he felt braver with every note he played.

But he kept it a secret. He wasn't ready to share his discovery—or his music—with anyone else. He wasn't sure if people would understand, and the idea of being laughed at made him nervous.

One afternoon, as he played a soft, dreamy tune, Mrs. Lacey peeked into the storage room. "Herald? Is that you?" she asked.

Herald jumped, his hands flying off the keys. "I… I was just… uh…"

Mrs. Lacey stepped closer, her eyes twinkling as she noticed the glowing keyboard. "What an incredible sound! Did you compose that?"

Herald nodded shyly.

"Herald, this is beautiful," Mrs. Lacey said warmly. "You've got something special here."

Herald felt a flicker of pride, but he quickly shook his head. "It's just… I mean, the keyboard is magical. It's not really me."

Mrs. Lacey smiled. "The keyboard might be special, but it's your fingers playing the music. Don't sell yourself short, Herald."

The Talent Show

A week later, Mrs. Lacey made an announcement during music class. "Students, the annual school talent show is coming up next month! If you have a talent—singing, dancing, magic tricks, anything—this is your chance to shine."

Herald's heart skipped a beat. The talent show sounded exciting, but the idea of performing made his palms sweaty.

"Herald," Mrs. Lacey said after class, "you should consider performing. Your music deserves to be heard."

Herald shook his head. "I can't, Mrs. Lacey. What if I mess up? What if everyone laughs at me?"

Mrs. Lacey knelt so they were at eye level. "Herald, everyone feels nervous about performing. But courage doesn't mean you're not afraid—it means doing it anyway. You've got something magical to share. Think about it."

Herald didn't answer, but her words stuck with him.

Facing His Fears

Over the next few weeks, Herald kept practicing in the storage room. The more he played, the more he thought about the talent show. He imagined standing on stage, the magical lights dazzling the audience.

But then he imagined freezing up, forgetting the notes, and hearing people whisper, "What's wrong with him?"

One afternoon, he told himself, "Maybe I'll just sign up and see what happens. If I change my mind, I don't have to go through with it." With shaky hands, Herald scribbled his name on the talent show sign-up sheet.

When the day of the show arrived, Herald sat backstage, his stomach doing flips. The other performers were excited, but Herald felt like he might faint. "Why did I think I could do this?" he thought.

Mrs. Lacey found him sitting in a corner, clutching his sheet music. "You're going to do great, Herald," she said with a reassuring smile. "Just focus on the music and let the rest take care of itself."

A Magical Performance

When it was Herald's turn, he wheeled the keyboard onto the stage, his legs trembling. The bright lights and the sea of faces in the audience made his heart race. He took a deep breath, closed his eyes, and placed his fingers on the keys.

The first note was soft and sweet, and the keyboard lit up with a golden glow. A hush fell over the audience. As Herald continued playing, the lights danced in rhythm with his melody, creating a mesmerizing display of color.

He played a cheerful, bouncy tune, making the audience tap their feet. Then he shifted to a slower, emotional piece, pouring his heart into every note. The entire gym erupted in applause when he finished with a triumphant, energetic finale.

Herald looked up, stunned. The audience was on their feet, clapping and cheering. For the first time, Herald felt something he hadn't expected: pride. He had done it. He had faced his fear and shared his music.

The Real Magic

After the show, Herald was surrounded by classmates, teachers, and even parents who wanted to congratulate him.

"That was incredible!" one boy said. "How did you get the lights to do that?"

"Your music was amazing!" another girl added. "I didn't know you could play like that!"

Herald blushed, but he couldn't stop smiling. "Thanks," he said shyly. "I've been practicing."

Mrs. Lacey approached him with a proud grin. "See? I told you your music deserved to be heard."

Herald nodded. "You were right, Mrs. Lacey. And I think… I think the magic wasn't just in the keyboard. It was in me all along."

Moral of the Story

Believing in yourself is the key to unlocking your potential.

Epilogue

As you close the final page of *You are an Amazing Boy*, remember that every story you've read is a reflection of the incredible qualities that make you who you are. Just like Herald, Eli, Lucas, and the other boys in these tales, you have the power to face challenges, show kindness, and make a difference in the world around you. Whether it's through bravery, creativity, or simply lending a helping hand, your unique strengths can shine bright and inspire others.

The adventures in this book may have ended, but your journey is just beginning. Carry these lessons with you as you dream big, embrace who you are, and keep discovering the amazing boy inside of you. The world is waiting for your story, and it's going to be extraordinary. Always believe in yourself—you are truly amazing!

You are an Amazing Girl
ISBN: 979-8300982416